LUMINOUS BLUE VARIABLES

LUMINOUS BLUE VARIABLES

AND OTHER MAJOR POEMS

Michelle Boisseau

BkMk Press
University of Missouri-Kansas City

BkMk Press
University of Missouri-Kansas City
5101 Rockhill Road
Kansas City, MO 64110

Executive Editor: Christie Hodgen
Managing Editor: Ben Furnish
Assistant Managing Editor: Cynthia Beard

Author photo by Thomas Stroik

BkMk Press wishes to thank intern Aidan Powers.

Partial funding for this project was provided by the Missouri Arts Council, a state agency.

For a complete list of donors, see page 141.

"Million Million." From *Among the Gorgons: Poems*. Tampa, Florida: University of Tampa Press, 2016. Reprinted with permission.

Credit: Michelle Boisseau. "A Reckoning" and "Across the Borderlands" from *A Sunday in God-Years*. Copyright © 2009 by The University of Arkansas Press. Reproduced with the permission of the University of Arkansas Press, www.uapress.com

Credit: Michelle Boisseau. "Two Winter Pictures", "Unending" and "Luminous Blue Variables" from *Trembling Air*. Copyright © 2003 by The University of Arkansas Press. Reproduced with the permission of the University of Arkansas Press, www.uapress.com

"Pink Swing," "Blood Sonata," "Cold Harbor," and "Likeness." From *Understory*. Northeaster University Press, 1996.

"The Gloss Avenue Ghost" and "The Night of the Breaking Glass." From *No Private Life*. Nashville, Tennessee: Vanderbilt University Press, 1990. Reprinted with permission.

Library of Congress Cataloging-in-Publication Data

Names: Boisseau, Michelle, 1955-2017, author.
Title: Luminous blue variables : and other major poems / Michelle Boisseau.

Description: Kansas City, MO : BkMk Press, [2021] | Summary: "This
   collection gathers poems from Michelle Boisseau's previous collections A
   Sunday in God Years, Trembling Air, Understory, No Private Life, and
   Indian Summer, as well as uncollected poems and interview excerpts"--
   Provided by publisher.
Identifiers: LCCN 2021015649 | ISBN 9781943491315 (paperback)
Subjects: LCGFT: Poetry.
Classification: LCC PS3552.O555 L86 2021 | DDC 811/.54--dc23
LC record available at https://lccn.loc.gov/2021015649

ISBN: 978-1-943491-31-5

In memory of Michelle Boisseau (1955-2017)

ACKNOWLEDGMENTS

Special thanks to Vanderbilt University Press and to the University of Arkansas Press for giving permissions to publish work that was first published by their presses:

"The Gloss Avenue Ghost" and "The Night of the Breaking Glass" first appeared in *No Private Life* (Vanderbilt University Press, 1990);

"Two Winter Pictures," "Unending," and "Luminous Blue Variables" first appeared in *Trembling Air* (The University of Arkansas Press, 2003);

"A Reckoning" and "Across the Borderlands, the Wind" first appeared in A Sunday in God-Years (The University of Arkansas Press, 2009).

Thanks, as well, to the following journals for publishing some of the poems in this volume:

Kentucky Poetry Review: "Fentress Creek"

Through the Gap: "The Enchantment"

Ark River Review: "Falling Into Place"

CONTENTS

Foreword   9

FROM *Among the Gorgons (2016)*
Million Million   13

FROM *A Sunday in God-Years (2009)*
A Reckoning   17
Across the Borderlands, the Wind   35

FROM *Trembling Air (2003)*
Two Winter Pictures   45
Unending   48
Luminous Blue Variables   51

FROM *Understory (1996)*
Pink Swing   59
Blood Sonata   62
Cold Harbor   65
Likeness   69

FROM *No Private Life (1990)*
The Gloss Avenue Ghost   87
The Night of the Breaking Glass   94

FROM *Indian Summer (1980)*
Indian Summer   99

Uncollected Poems
Fentress Creek   115
The Enchantment   118
Falling Into Place   120
Some Will Tell You   123

Interviews   125

FOREWORD

Michelle worked on her poetry until the day she died. Her lung cancer, debilitating as it was, never lessened her passion for her art. In her last weeks, besides revising several new poems, Michelle started to compile a volume of *New and Selected Poems*. She passed away, unexpectedly quickly, on November 15, 2017, leaving her final volume, sadly, unfinished.

Months later I shared the volume with our daughter Anna, who noticed, with some dismay, that "Luminous Blue Variables" (one of Anna's favorite poems by her mother) wasn't included in the collection. I tried to explain that Michelle had wanted the volume to include only short lyrical poems. But Anna's concerns got me to think about how dazzling all of Michelle's long poem are. It is in her long poems that Michelle best displays her rare gift for bringing poetry, history, science, and philosophy together (a gift Michelle was very modest about).

I can't thank Anna enough for inspiring this volume of Michelle's long poems. Having these poems speak to one another allows us to overhear celestial conversations.

I would like to thank the editors at BkMk Press—Ben Furnish, Robert Stewart, and Christie Hodgen—for working so hard on bringing this volume to life. Finally, I would like to thank Lindsey Weishar for preparing the early versions of this book.

—Thomas Stroik

FROM

Among the Gorgons

(2016)

Million Million

=1,000,000,000,000

A trillion seconds ago we danced to bone flutes
The Mountain Marries the Rain. Like petals
on a black bough sentences burst from us
and we hit on handy words right and left.
We scratched the walls deep so the stampede

leapt in firelight, but one of us a million million
seconds ago had sung a song or dug a grave
on this side of the globe. No canyons recorded
the wooly monsters that the Osage-orange tree
still longs for, dangling its softball size fruit

each summer for hungers that never come
while the locust tree bristles with daggers
against eons of empty treats. A billion seconds ago
I ripped through Ohio and half a dozen boyfriends
in two million seconds and you spread a quilt

with your first wife by the Tidal Basin. Mozart,
cherry trees a pink mist. On the high bench
sat nine judicious scholars. Authorities reported
the answer to world hunger was fish
for they were numberless. A thousand million

seconds ago all of our families were still alive,
except our children, yet to be desired. In twenty-five
years we've been apart only a million seconds
and in a million more I'll be driving you home
through an enormous day. Put the thousand count

sheet on the bed, in a million seconds
        I'll be home with you.

FROM

A Sunday in God-Years

(2009)

A Reckoning

1. The Debt

To the two strong trees, the well-screwed hooks, the
       ropes, what does the hammock owe?

The portico, to the cut stone?

The groaning board, the roast, the butter, and gloaming
       jams appear to speak in a register beyond dog
       whistles. Who can hear forests and cattle, briars
       and caramelized steam?

What does the storm sculling across the continent owe
       the ocean?

Second-growth? At least third, maybe fourth. In the
       woods the developer's crew stands around a hole.
       The idling machines say hurry, hurry. Someone
       clinks a shovel at something in the backhoe's
       bucket. Tibia. Someone sizes up how many and
       much. Glances are exchanged, tamping down,
       tamping down, and the machines start up again.

In the courthouse, books as big as tables speak in lacy
       script. What do you owe when you find your
       name on a parchment deed?

2. Ruminator

Don't misunderstand.
I am the cow. This is my field,
my golden meadow. This my murky pond
where I ruminate and switch flies.

I eat the grass. The dry seeds skitter,
meander on the breeze and drop
from birds. Birds pick at bronze
droppings in the grass I eat.

Don't continue
to misunderstand there is a cow,
there is a field.

I am the field, the wavering meadow
I eat, the murky pond
I shamble to and drink,
flanks steaming.

———

No one can remember
the forests, forests without
understory, looming tip to tip.
The green shade.

No one remembers the trees
dragged away
became lumber and great fleets
went under.

In the morning the flat ocean
glowing under the sun
and nothing new

———

No one remembers the ship
limped into Charleston, a fired cannon
announced the arrival and a pilot boat
started out, but the harbor was already
awake to the shipment. Before dawn
they could smell it coming.

La Rochelle. Calabar. St. Kitts,
Providence. Liverpool. Richmond.

Clover to clover bloom, port to port,
bees gathering honey, the great fleets
sailed round and great cities rose.

The estates are still famous.
The good graces, ringing forges, teas
under lock and key, nimble servants.

———

Cows dot the lawns. Around a bend
chimneys sprout from a mountain
of roofs. Windows slowly amber
in the evening sun. Behind
a line of trees, the cabins
lengthen in the shadow tide.

Are you arriving in the carriage?
Or around back in a wagon?

Imported, like the cow or honey bee,
sweet potato or daffodil, soon you belong
where you find yourself. Children,
grandchildren. Broken staves nailed
over a chink. Sugar in the silver service. Gold

leaves curing in the barns.
And the cow lumbers into the pond,
tears sour grass and murks the water.

3. No Trespassing. Violators Will Be Prosecuted, etc.

A road of industrial gravel staggers
under the locked gate I climb, under
the second gate I swing beneath.

Drizzle sticks like cotton lint to junk trees and scrub.

And around the bend, a clearing, opening onto ...
Nope, not The House Where They Lived!

No be-lilaced cellar hole buzzing
like a hornet's nest with ancient meaning.
Nothing to weep over. No granite knees—
even the rocks aren't local, trucked in, dumped.

Instead, big as an airplane hangar,
a garage for backhoes and spreaders turns up
where the big house might have stood.

How many cabins would they have required
for the three score people they held
as slaves? This time next year
the trees will have been knocked aside
like incidents and the driveways poured.

I cowl my camera as the rain picks up
and video the view they didn't have—
across the Appomattox smoke sputters from
a single-wide trailer—thumbtack stuck in a tree.

4. Meanwhile

The year Whistler was born and Coleridge died;
the year Lincoln rode into Springfield
a fresh assemblyman, and hansom cabs
of bachelors began speeding around London;
the year Pushkin's *Queen of Spades*
appeared, an ink-smeared boy Whitman
set type against agitators, McCormick
parented his reaper, and mobs combed
Philadelphia burning out blacks
and abolitionists; the year what's now
Oklahoma, Kansas, and Nebraska
became Indian Territory and ragged
bands of Shawnee were run out of Ohio;
the year Emerson struck the gold vein
of his style and fell in love with Lydia;
the year, on the quiet, with old spelling books,
Frederick Douglass conducted school
for fellow slaves was the year my mother's
great-grandfather, a boy in Pennsylvania,
studied his Bible by daylight and lamplight
and my father's great-grandfather wrote out
a notice and trotted the dusty roads
of Virginia to place it in the paper:

5. Reward

$20 REWARD.—Ran away from the subscriber on the night of the 29th of June, a negro man named GIBSON, about 23 or 24 years of age, five feet eight or nine inches high, rather spare, of a dark complexion, very polite when spoken to. He carried off all his clothing, consisting of three pair of cotton, one pair of dark yarn, and a pair of green corduroy pantaloons, one blue cloth coat, and two hats; one a good wool hat, and the other a fur hat, with crape around it. I suspect he is either in Richmond, where he has been heretofore hired in a Tobacco Factory, or in the neighborhood of Mr. Richard Gregory's, near the Half-way House, where his father lives. I will give twenty dollars for the said Negro man if delivered to me near Chesterfield Court House, or committed to Jail, so That I can obtain him again.

      July 4.   PETER F. BOISSEAU.

               —*Richmond Enquirer*, July 11, 1834

6. The Subscriber

The dipper dropped by the well, a footprint
among the climbing beans, the uncertain figure
inked in the mirror before the lamp is lit,
everywhere I look I read his signature.
A fellow loping along the road, his shadow
bouncing beside him. Or when I waited
for the ferry, across the river his sad
eyes and watchful smile printed on another boy's face.
He befriends the shadows of trees. His gait,
that slouch hat and his way of crushing
the brim when something strikes him strange.
I even stared at a white man at supper
in a tavern. The thorough way the man
licked his spoon called up my Gibson's manner.
Though every Negro here to the Half-way
House says they can't say they've seen him and can't
recollect the last time they did, I know
he's out there, bedded down in the woods, maybe
sidling into the barn when it storms, owing
his meals to raided orchards and stealing
toward our windows to haunt us as we sleep.

Expecting no luck like every other time,
I'm rounding the corner to the factory
and nearly leap out of my boots. It's him,
stretched bold as you please across some sacks,
and I'm on him and he's hollering, *Mercy,*
Mercy as my cane snaps across his back,
my foot greets his head. When I go to turn
him over, his arm feels too beefy, too slack
the skin around his neck. Blood is darkening

the stream of piping along his collar. Something like
Gibson's coat. Two boys loading lumber in a cart
catch me looking around and style
themselves reading the grain in a board.
Sleeping in the day. This one was a laggard.

7. Catalogue

On the old map, roads end at the county line,
rivers snap like the branches in an ice storm.
A gray blank islands the county
the way a halo of disappearance conceals

the man who fled a Boisseau farm.
Escaped? Captured? Sold south?
Undocumented. Rivers of unknowns
wash out his trail, leaving me the dry

marshes of archives. Holes and time-traps.
I wander this heated, clacking terrain
(microfilm flapping on the take-up reel)
collecting paper triumphs:

the soundings taken from land patents
(640 acres in 1756),
the reckonings of census and slave lists
(1500 acres in 1840, 56 slaves),

the sick victories from deciphering
the loops and strokes of handwritten wills:

8. Two Wills in Old Virginia

Of Sarah H. Baugh Boisseau, 1820: "I give and bequeath unto my daughter Priscilla H. Boisseau for and during the term of her natural life the following slaves, to wit, Matt, Tom, Busheba, and Little Suey and her infant child Iris, also the large bed, bedstead and bureau in my chamber."

Of Priscilla Hill Boisseau, 1856, "I give and bequeath to my grand-daughther Elizabeth R. Gibbs, my Negro girl Emily and her child Elie together with the future increase of the said slave Emily to his and her heirs forever."

9. Apologies

only account for that which they do not alter.
—Benjamin Disraeli

The traffic of a sentimental novel
guides the runaway Gibson
past drunk patrols, through snake-rippling
swamps riddled with the ironic slow

butterfly. Days of running till below the Falls
he spots a British vessel in the fog,
on deck a disciple of Wilberforce
avid to smuggle him cinematically

across an ocean brimming with moon-roads,
inalienable rights and speaking tours.
Freedom is hard-won, but done. Sizzling platters
are carried in. Grab a chair and sit down.

Good gracious! Look at all this food.
Everyone finds a place at the table. Captain
and cook, shipper and shipped. Gibson's
great-great-grandchildren. And Little Suey's.

And me, grandchild who makes herself the hero
since she's the teller of this tale. I writhe
and what of it? How can I begin to recount
the sins, a million ships on every ocean?

10. Spear-Side and Distaff

The new curls from the old and the old rots
underfoot. Whoever came up with *tree?*
when a family's a swamp, messy woods
good for getting lost, for stillness lost
in the clack of branches. What's that? Nothing.
And nothing again. Echoes, the soundings
of falling things, skirmishes of the unseen.

No one but me has come this way lately,
touched the runnels of bark, smelled the sweetness
of decay and slapped impediments
glinting like spider silk along the trail.
From him the slope of my nose, from her
freckles. And who's responsible for these
lead moods? Boisseau, Parham, Hill,

Bradley, Fitzpatrick, Holt, Holmes,
and I'm square in seventeenth-century
Virginia where the hush grows huge and sulky
as a scolded jury. And the evidence?
Impurely circumstantial. The circumstances?
Dangling husks that blur the branches, the way
the fallen cushion and obliterate.

11. Brown Study

Here three shades of white exchange thoughts.
The trampled snow talks to the icy river
and the low sky answers back. As it thaws,
the border muddies underfoot. Rocks shift

their attention and give way though each night's
general freeze shuts them down, a border town
under siege. Sky and ice, water and ice,
land and ice. It's fine to think we were formed

from mud. It's fine pictures of rivers favor
them bounding toward us (because the retreating
river is too sad, it runs away, waves
turn their backs on us). That the sky is fleet

is helpful. The earth turns. Rivers run like people,
far and fast as they can to taste the sea.

12. Field Guide to North American Guilt

Outcroppings of the oldest forms
have weathered into mountain stubs,
blunt incisors of a blind dog
the household skirts around. The worn

hill spills its gravel which is chewed
and smoothed in riverbeds and sported
along, burrs on the fur of currents,
and with silt, shells, bugs, tracks, and spume

laid in oceans. Impressed with time. Scarred.
Or driven deep under to boil.
And sometimes, rarely, it is tamed,
expressed like rubies from feldspar,

the clear, crimson crystal of shame.

13. Before the Age of Aerial Bombardment

Shenandoah Valley, October, 1864

Detail, abstraction, creation.
In the flying dream I glide above the scorch
and guns, brooding over the fields
as I form the world from an old battle map.

Burnt Mill   *J. Howell*   School-House
Widow Stickley   ROSSER 11. P.M.

A river squiggles inside the tighter squiggles
of contour lines. Arrows and penpoints
quicken farmstead and depot, commander
and camp, chimney stump. I perch a moment
at 4 AM where the squashed buttery
moon glints off his buttons or his horse
clicks a rock at Cupp's Ford, and it is time

for my Confederate great-grandfather
to get gutshot. And waste away, linger
three years—*the wound still suppurating*—
then leave his widow with child
who has one child. Therefore, writhing reckoner,
I ride this map like a flying carpet
and start the world for them to end again.

14. Gibson

Though you try to puppet me,
what happened to me is not

for you to know. You know it was
a Sunday night I fled. You

know (or so says U.S.
Naval Observatory's

website) the moon, a waning
crescent, rose after midnight

and civil twilight ended
at 8:06. You can lie

on the floor and try macro-
imagining me from drained swamps,

Capitol dome, stacked stones, orchards
(my far-stretched hand even moves

your first spoonful of peaches)
and micro-imagining

the stench of fear, summer woods,
hunger, slapping vines, hard moons

on my shoeless feet, the bite
of roots as I steal away

on the long wire of longing
which hooks itself one end to

your gut, hooks the other end
to lover, brother, father,

open ocean. Longing you
know. Seven generations,

you know of, engendering
generations. Do the math.

15. Eighteenth-Century Boisseau Farmhouse

after a WPA photo

Leafless tree shadow scribbles the walls
and shadows of deflated bushes flood
the yard, an arrogant silver squalor
so pitted and clumped it seems a crowd
had barged about, then despaired of raising
a response from such a blank and pointless house.

Bare weatherboard of equivocal
color, snaggle-toothed shutters.
The place couldn't look better
for how bad it looks. Mythic,
Faulknerian. With a satisfying smack
of the cartoon. A place you'd discover

a goat enjoying the taste of mantel.
Shirts tugged from an offstage clothesline
and flung beside the swayback steps
turn out to be chickens, a couple
strutting roosters, and a lone peahen.
Someone has been working here,

patching the roof? carrying it off?
A long glaring ladder meets, tweezers-like,
its crisp leaning shadow—the two long legs
of a huge being who's about to stride
over the fields and trees, over the excellent
fires made when old wood starts to burn.

Across the Borderlands, the Wind

My present field of consciousness is a centre surrounded by a
fringe that shades insensibly into a subconscious of more.
—William James

Fringe planet. Shifty river. Bright shade.

The notes between the notes we hear
loud as the bird song. Bright shade
then morning blaze. This time of day
our shadows grow us tall and even
the seams between close-laid stones
in the dawn street are touched,
light-honed and articulated.

Mountain range and threadbare frontier.
Foray, skirmish, raid. By war, treaty,
algebra and surveyors in knee britches.
Stay out of my yard! City limits, state line,
double electric fence, high wall,
and watchtower where bored soldiers
insult each other's sisters on schedule.

———

The eastern woods give way to the long grass
that gives way to the short-grass prairie,
gumbo lily, whistle of meadow lark
riding and falling on the wind.

Last gas for ninety-three miles.

———

I'm half asleep as I watch them crossing
the border into Kansas. Coming out
of the night woods, they're the dark
coming apart, the avant dark, ahead

of a dawn ordinary to an old man
who presses a cheek against his cow's flank.
Warm milk threads his fingers, a breeze
drags the dust around the farmyard

where Quantrill's raiders ride in.
In earshot of the town they'll burn, they don't
shoot him like the nine others but club him
with the butt-end of a Sharps carbine.
A flash of wood, the sleek shaft gripped,
and I look away, again the aerial view,
the stream of riders like the wind through grass

as they gallop up the streets of Lawrence.
The tent tops of the recruit encampment
(a plot now shaded by a parking structure)—
I hover till they're the size of screw heads,
and the pursuit and slaughter and fire
jumping roof to roof become a gray
business of graphite and margins
gradated by the thickets of sleep.

————

The tideline makes the gull bold
to snatch a sandwich from a child's hand
and the sandpiper anxious,
drilling its shining self on the wet berm.

Wetlands, momentary land
of leggy tadpoles.

————

When they was kids, him and his sister
would beg their daddy to drive down

State Line Road, and they'd stretch out
in the back seat of the Hudson,

heads in Kansas, feet in Missouri
where the peachy moon was rising.

——◆——

Ordinance and algebra. Along the dammed
and channeled river where I grew up,
you could look down from Eden Park
on Kentucky. The bare rooftops

and vertiginous spires of the poor
former slave state offended
the good sense we had to be born
in Ohio. And yet the crooked smile,

like someone who'd brushed up
against a splendid outlaw,
Dad would make a wistful crack
about his grandfather's rumored
riches, slaves lost in old Virginia.

——◆——

Latching on to a likely host
wafting past, it sucks a door
out of the cell wall: not alive but living
off life, the virus attacks passively

like in-laws. Next thing you know
you're tripping over their suitcases
and they've broken up your bed
for fires under their roaring kettles.

——◆——

A note pinned to a dead jayhawker,
"You come to hunt bushwackers.
Now you ar skelpt." When the worst

border-war guerilla was killed,
Bloody Bill Anderson, they reported
eleven human scalps fluttered like ribbons

from his bridle band. Tucked in his watch case
a lock from his buxom wife. Townsfolk
lined up to have a picture with the corpse.

———•———

Oxbow lake.
When the river

shifted, it left
an elbow of water

and this here
part of the state

was stranded
and stubbornized.

———•———

The way smoke rising from many fires
is blown in tangles and scuds
like a blanket dragged across a floor
of rooftops and competing spires, the chiming

from churches on one side of the Green Line
wed the singing from minarets
on the other as the crackle of vespas
and blaring Euro hiphop tried to amp up

the coolness factor of the strobing stores
of the South Nicosia shopping district
that gave way to the silences of warehouses,
workshops where a few machines whined

under low lights. When I walked past,
Western woman with a water bottle,
workers glanced up then back to the making
of laminated furniture for seashore condos,

then a dead end at the Green Line, barrel
barricades, streets of weeds, walls crumbling
like cake and feral cats wending through
the way looping thoughts wake a sleeper.

Trees eagered from de-glazed windows.
I heard a cough. At my elbow, wedged
into a slit of shade, a young man with a gun
and a water bottle—a sweating sunburned blond

in a UN uniform—we'd startled each other,
and now humbled by the heat, befuddled
by a goofy sense of guilt, we scrambled
to nod obliquely and look away.

———

At the last station before Holland,
a voice on the speakers announced,
"Alle Juden heraus." The train hissed,
doors slammed, and because Bertha,
the oldest, had the presence of mind

to warn her sisters to sit still, they made
Amsterdam, and later the Twin Cities,
where they lived to old age. Their neighbors—

who'd obeyed, gathered up their coats
and stepped off—were not heard from again.

———

Drips and drains. Late night, deep
into that frayed frontier, the ICU's
screens measuring his body's forecast

in slim crests and dips: Still, still, still,
there's comfort even in the steady
mechanical breathing, the stalwart

ventilator leashed to my brother,
the terrible comfort I will take
from time slipping at the door.

———

Ticking off centuries like seconds,
the great slow plates clutch

and shift intent as lovers, seas open,
mountains climb and fold. Elephants

broke fences, monkeys raced
for high ground: everybody except people

knew it was coming. For weeks after
the quake, the earth rang like a bell.

———

From a dock on a lake
on an island in a lake
I dive into the stars,
scatter them and gather them
between my arms and legs,
then watch them heal themselves

in place. Venus rebounds
on the water, the wet dock,
the low islands of my breasts:
we're all in a reflective mood.

Even centuries past the fringe
planets like Pluto, the sun,
dim as the last
gas station we left miles back,
tugs and grips,
oh, the gravitas of edges.

———

When he blew clean
the borderline between stone

and body grown from stone
Michelangelo's eyelashes

were dusted with desire
like the hair of a honey bee.

———

The tiny wellsprings dimpling
the ridges of our fingertips mist

the air that touches us. Lying in bed,
tracing a vein that crosses your arm,

I'm the ocean in love with the sky.
Seamless ripples, a rise and response,

clouds are the trade of touch, exchange
rate of kisses. Never, *There,* or *Once*

and for all though we sweat and murmur,
That should keep you fucked a while.

FROM

Trembling Air

(2003)

Two Winter Pictures

Très Riches Heures of Jean, Duke of Berry

1. *January*: A Very Fine Time, Indeed

Inside the rare book, a painting, in the painting
    a tapestry of knights crashing and falling
    in a cascade of helmets. It hangs in the banquet hall
where homely Duc de Berry, among his retinue and gold plates,

welcomes guests from the cold: *approche approche* he says
    in gold-leaf. Hands stretched toward their patron or toward
    the fire they painted behind him, the Limbourg
brothers enter their masterpiece with their wives. In crafty gags

we can only guess at, the brothers set before us
    a scene that translates *Noblesse oblige* as *Be generous*
    to artists. Small feathery dogs stroll companionably
    among platters of woodcock on the damasked table.

A knightly drinker is dwarfed by the gold bowl he drains
and the duke eclipsed by the glowing brocade
    only the rich could wear. Somehow the cocky courtiers
    deeply slighted the painters: from cup bearer (wearing one spur!)

and carver, the hilts of their daggers jut out just so—
pizzles prompted for coupling, but no likely place disposed.

2. *February*: Crying with a Loaf of Bread in Your Hands

Leaving the shelter in January's
    lush illumination,
we come to skim-milk snow,
    pewter sky, seedy rations

pigeons pick from farmyard droppings.
    But through beehive and kindling
in bundles, sheepcote and a donkey
    driven to a distant village,

the painting shows a peasant life
    that might content a duke.
Through cut-away walls of the quaint
    cottage he could look

at clothes hung to dry by a modest fire
    that warms three figures.
One is a woman in a blue dress
    that she lifts demurely

to her knees. Behind her are men—
    we see when we look close—
for they've hitched their wet tunics
    above their thighs to expose

dangling genitals. A lampoon for—or on—
    a childless patron? Or on her?
But she's learned to ignore the antics
    of her husband's celibate (since poor

and landless) younger brothers. Farmhands
    on the farm that's never theirs,
they fling seed, flail grain, gather fruit
    and never hope to marry;

even a rude encounter in town
        takes hard cash. End of the road
for their genes' long lines
        fizzling in the dangling stones

they tease her with, in that damp house
        on a long-ago day
imagined with fresh paint by living men
        while the matter of our own making

coiled in thousands of nameless strangers
        with the dumb luck to escape
siege, plague, prison, famine, and fire
        just long enough to mate

with another sturdy soul, giving
        us the length of our bones, the black
in our hair, a weakness for salt,
        and this strange run of luck.

Unending

We went to trouble ourselves in a place
of heavy occasion. It was a wet March dawn.
Sleet stuck pins to our coats as we scaled
the subway stairs to former East Berlin,
then got lost among new Mercedes showrooms
and buildings blasted out for fifty years: the fall
of communism as the spring of capitalism.
Our hotel eyed a domed church humbled
by construction cranes. They hung over it
like checkmarks, a child hunched beneath a board
that chalks up his infractions.

At the Institute, an ice storm of resentment
broke between old East and old West Berliners,
and my husband spilled his research
in a rush of English that rankled them the more.
Then came the luncheon. *Hackepeter
vom Schwein* or *Schlactplatte?* Both
were stiff mounds under tarps of gravy.

———

A cold mist filled the air but didn't fall.
I managed to pry off a raisin-sized bit
of the Wall though it was fenced against vandals.
Beside it, in former free Berlin, the ruins
of Gestapo Headquarters. A place
of heavy occasion getting heavier.
That's the way it goes, straw upon straw.

To say I can't bear anymore, we've walked days,
the children are shaking with hunger,
means the machine guns come out, means

there's blood in the baby's stool.
Then your shoes get stolen.

———

When my friend Achille was a boy in Italy,
he didn't cry when the fascists marched
into the square a pregnant villager
and shot her for letting a partisan
steal a chicken. He didn't cry
when the retreating army blew up the station
and limbs and bits of button rained and drizzled.

It was the cart-horse that made him cry.
Tail shooing off flies, it had been waiting in harness
to be tapped with a whip when the explosion
lifted it up and smashed it like an apple
against the bricks of the telegraph office.

And there it hung for all to see.
Though bodies and parts of bodies
littered the station yard, and those still alive
moaned (*for the love of God help me*),
the people pointed at that dead animal—
that took no sides, that wanted only grass—
and they cried. And forty years later
Achille's tears slipped loose as he told me.

———

And so it was not the ruined detention cells
where the Gestapo dumped prisoners
after interrogation. It wasn't descending
to the makeshift museum in the cellar kitchens,
nor the photographs of face after face
of those who entered there. But one face.

The word "Wisconsin" jumped out.
My husband's home state, dairy farms, broad minds,
Poles, Germans, and good government.
The caption: *Mildred Harnack-Fish (1902-1943)*
in 1942 while in Gestapo detention,
a UW lit prof who'd married
a founder of Red Orchestra, the resistance group.

She was looking calmly at her Nazi photographer.
She'd pulled her dark hair back tight,
as I do when about to start a job, and appeared
yet unhurt though I read she was tortured
and the next winter executed. Around me
old bricks, display cases, some school kids
reading about the burning of the synagogue.

Under glass the open volume of Goethe
she had with her when arrested. A priest
who visited her had saved it. In the margin,
in a grave dark hand, her translation reads:
All is given by the Gods, the unending Ones,
To those whom They love—They withhold nothing,
All joys, unendingly,
All pain, unendingly, They withhold nothing.

Luminous Blue Variables

If the stars should appear one night in a thousand years,
how would men believe and adore; and preserve for many
generations the remembrance of the city of God which had
been shown! But every night come out these envoys of beau-
ty, and light the universe with their admonishing smile.

—Emerson

Inside the hollow rock, following the sound
of water, still we climbed, he first and I second,
until I glimpsed through an opening

some of the beautiful cargo the sky carries.
And then I climbed out to see the stars again.
As I leaned back, taking long drinks of air

like someone draining a cold bucket,
my eyes opened farther and let the stars
behind the stars come forward. As the quiet

became a steady throb, I realized
he was gone. Though I looked for him feelingly
among the stiff shadows, starlit

rocks and bushes, I knew he had gone
at the moment of my deepest looking,
gone like a ship on the horizon,

a dimpling, an echo, then beyond

———

the bronze gong of my father's voice

———

If we could see far-red, infrared,
and ghostly ultraviolet, the ground would glow

with them, the sky would shower them.
While we stand on tiptoe looking out,

our eyes trained by common colors
borne by our sun, invisible powers
are riding the waves—are the waves—
gliding toward us, through us humming

as the killing glances shot by stars
darker and sharper roll off our foamy shield

———•—•———

my father's voice sounded on the long waves
of radio, late into the night, rolling

———•—•———

"Power is only Pain
Stranded, thro' Discipline"

———•—•———

The bland afternoon, which seems a direct
plane of light, a window, misdirects me.
For indirection is the way
the world comes. The colors

of plants, sky, stones are spectral
signatures. We write our names in waves.
And the day's blue name blanks out the night.
But through the glare, through glass,

through sheetrock and shingles
the unseen envoys roll, fast and fretted—
silent whistle that makes the dog moan—
or long-sloped radio waves, postcards

mailed from the beginning of time.
We crouch at a slot in the door

———

"Why, Mister, we get you better than some of those Atlanta
stations"

———

late into the night, top of the hour,
his voice tolled out the news—
holdup, police chase, river drowning—
rolled from nightstand, through car window
gliding under streetlights, rippled north
across cornfields, into Michigan and Canada,
and south, broadcast to truckers
bouncing on I-75, to Florida by morning
with static and starlight dimmed

———

"The nine-pound meteorite crashed through the roof of a home occu-
pied by Mrs. E. Hulitt Hodges in Sylacauga, Ala. at 1:00 P.M. C.S.T. on
Nov. 30, 1954. It bounced off a console radio in her living room and
hit her hip, which was bruised enough to require hospitalization."

———

And as he came near that city
a sudden light glowed around him,
a light leaping from the sky,
and as he dropped to the ground
Saul heard a voice saying

———

static and starlight dimmed
above the parked car where the radio

was tuned to the final innings
of the game we'd skipped,
I drew squiggles on the window, bored
with the boy and making out,
and at the top of the hour, I turned the volume up—
arson fire in Avondale, a shooting in Covington—
disasters to daunt my date from the suburbs,
rolling through us in the dark
on the disciplined voice of an errant man,
that easy beauty of my father's baritone

———

"A light will suddenly appear. It quickly grows intensely bright,
but it hardly seems to move. That is because it is headed right
for the witness."

———

She leans back inside the rain of gold,
bending and dipping so it splashes
against her skin. Looking up Danaë sees
she has become a tower of light that reaches
as far up as the sun reaches down.
When mortals are struck by the more-
than-mortal, an echo bounces back and back

———

the easy beauty of his baritone fading,
he was happiest with a pack of cash
and a piano bar when someone asked him to sing,
crooner with a drink and a bad line
of credit, in his wallet a shrunken xerox
of his daughter's poem, sad poem
about him gone dim and dwindling,
and over the orbit of the glass—

where a planet bobbed on a toothpick axis—
he struck the bronze gong of his baritone

———

"But, after all, death runs in that family."

———

Forgive me I have called all you stars
false names—china chips, nailheads, punctures,

blue jean rivets, glitter—I was afraid
your grandeur would diminish me. And you

blue stars, luminous blue variables
who live hot and die quickest,

you show me when the greatest collapse,
it is as if one man and all his mock gravity

had been compressed into a single cell's
smallest locket where it throbs,

rolling out invisible messages.
Only when I was looking up,

the sky opening at my looking,
did I feel him gone and wholly unhurt.

One life is so small its story fits everywhere,
and even when the life comes to disaster,

the waves climb and crest and climb.
History is daylight, night eternity.

FROM

Understory

(1996)

Pink Swing

1.

I play architect to my stepdaughter's heart,
drawing a house to her heart's desire:
"That's your and daddy's room. Now make a red one

for me. Now one for mommy." (I comply, I comply.
If this is a test, I will pass it.)
"Now a little house for the cat,

and put the pink swing in the tree."
When I've finished—making sure every door
has a knob, each window a curtain—

she spreads the picture on the floor and sings to it.
She has us where she wants us, under one
newshingled roof, and means to make us happy.

2.

Months after she's gone back, we're still finding her:
a bouquet of crayons under sofa cushions,
green spool of a Tinkertoy, farmyard ladder
the length of a pencil. This side of custody,
our affections go in safekeeping.

Give up the yellow anklet you found
clinging to the sheets. With each thing
we drop in a shoe box—wooden chicken, scuffed
baby that fits in the pocket—we find we're singing
the song she taught us: "Oh, where have you been

Billy Boy, Billy Boy? Oh, where
have you . . . ?" Her voice darts
around our heads like a dragonfly
on a thread, a bead of mercury rolling
inside a bottle given a feverish child.

3.

Before you punch the eleven numbers
that call your daughter up, you take a deep breath

and swing yourself into thin air. What can you say
to a small child through a telephone?

What of yourself can you push through a thousand
miles of switches that she might catch?

She's too young to listen long, one ear to your voice seeping
from the housing, the other taking in

the clatter of her mother listening from another room.
When you say, "Katie, the cat is sleeping

in the flowers, they want you to pick them,"
how can she believe you? She can see for herself

it's starting to snow again, a shaggy sleet
that ticks like static against the window.

4.

Flutter kicking up our legs to make room
for herself, one morning she jumped
into bed with us and said, "Hey guys,
I'm back!" as if sleep were a place
night carried her, milkweed

fluff lofted through the dream trees.
Waking up these days, where does she imagine you?
The polka dot that shrank
into the road the morning she hopped
from foot to foot in the parking lot?

Is the world to her smooth
as a cartoon, one seamless surface
then the door pops open
with you in it? You're thrown back
on yourself at age four, fishing inside
the great box of flimsy clues.

But the smell of graham crackers, the stiffness
of church shoes, don't reveal her
and they can't convince you
she knows you're coming back.

5.

Disc of pink plastic dangling
from the rope, monkey swing we hung
last August for her visit. The thinnest breeze
pushes it above the grassless spot. Pendent
from the branch that lets it swing
but keeps it tethered, all it can do

is describe its small territory
in squiggles and arcs, to jerk and dance
at the end of its line, as if trying
to escape, to slip the rope and fly off
even if just to plummet like a waterlogged
star into the hedges. How awful is childhood—

the child only potential on a rope. When it rains,
the water runs from her. When it snows,
she wears a skirt of it. And every blessed minute
there's a chittering in the broad sky
that seems to mean something,
a something that means to exclude her.

Blood Sonata

Plump envelope, baby
folded twice in flannel,
tucked into a glass box
(though she won't wait for kisses
to wake her), and wheeled in
to us, the nurse's crepe soles
lightly smacking the polished floor.
The bed sits me up and you
lift her to me and settle her
above the incision. Unwrap the crystal
flutes you've brought from home
and let's knock them into music
as you kick your shoes off
and scoot in beside me.

And if she bear a maid child,
then she shall be unclean
two weeks … and whosoever toucheth
her bed shall wash his clothes
and bathe himself
and be unclean until the evening …
and if any man lie
with her at all
and her flowers
be upon him he shall be unclean
for seven days and all
the bed whereon
he lieth shall be unclean.
—Leviticus

On the operating table they curtained
me off from myself and I played along,
pretending to be blinded while I watched
them work in the silver hood
of the hanging lamp, a little window
to my body. The surgeon's hand
crossed my belly and presto,
a widening smile of blood the nurse
patted with gauze. Then the hood
was shifted, the anesthetics
coiled in my head and I saw only
a white corner of the room, an envelope flap,
until the pediatrician appeared with her,
blue, gluey, and blinking.

———

The female is
as it were
a deformed male.
—Aristotle

———

No wonder the riddle tripped them up:
Not of woman born. Not of woman
as in not borne through
the narrow canal? The bearded
physician scooping the baby out
steaming into the damp room.
Faces flickering by the peat fire,
the hushed women dabbed the blood and gel
from the soft head, the toes. Only afterwards
do they turn to the one laid out
on the plank table (not of woman
born, for woman no longer?)

and tuck her back inside herself, wind her body
like a spindle in fresh linen.

———

Contact with it turns
new wine sour, crops touched
by it become barren, grafts
die, seeds in gardens
are dried up, the fruit
of the trees falls off,
the bright surface of mirrors
in which it is merely reflected
are dimmed, the edge of steel,
and the gleam of ivory
are dulled, the hives of bees
die, even bronze and iron
are at once seized by rust.
—Pliny the Elder

———

Where's the shame for it?
A shame instead to flush away
this bright excess flowing
from me without first stopping
to steady myself against the dizzy tiles
and admire the red tethers tumbling
through the watery world, the blood
pooling at the bottom like a dropped robe.
Wet plums in a white bowl
and I the orchard. How could I feel shame
in the fact of it? as the sky's
a blue fact stretched tight as silk
above the hospital and the green facts
of pines pouring down the hillsides.

Cold Harbor

The traffic pulls its sleeves across the lake
of sleep that inches toward me then rolls away
like mercury. The moon is shrunk
to a china chip in the trees, baffled
by the falling sky. Nights like this the day
won't leave me alone. The wheels
of a grapefruit sliced for breakfast bob up
somehow with the student who wept in my office
embarrassed, patting her wet face
with the report of her blood work
while I dabbed her shoulder and fumbled around.
And what about these crickets? One under our bed now.
Are they nesting in the floorboards? We've found
the knuckle-sized singers on book-spines,
along the ceiling, behind the doorjambs,
creaking through the house until we think
the woods will drown us all.

And tonight in the day's arbitrary flotsam
a black man piling onto a wooden stretcher
gray rags and bones, the Union dead at Cold Harbor.
A picture in a book of pictures, the glossy
guide to the traveling exhibit
we couldn't travel to. I don't think
this man has slept all week either.
His face is shining in the heat, the gray field
shining back at him. I can't see
a tree for miles, a cup of shade
where he might talk low with the others,
shirts and spades that blur
behind the grim stack where he poses.
No trees.

I almost want to wake you up.
Weren't the trees several stories high
that spring we visited the battlefield?
How could they have grown so fast?

In the time it takes to drive the length of this town
from the Quickstop to the tobacco warehouse,
in the time it takes to wash the fixative
over a collodion print,
five acres of Virginia fields went blue
with fallen Union soldiers, a loud
twitching sea, 7,000. Those still alive
in the crossfire scratched out trenches
with bayonet and tin cup and spoon.
The luckiest had friends who dragged them back,
dribbled water across their lips,
and wrote home for them afterwards.
They'd expected the worst. The night before,
they'd sewn inside their collars
scraps of paper with their names and regiments.
The unlucky lay where they dropped. Three days
of moaning, then the long quiet under the sun.
October fogged the fogged faces.
December shagged the timothy and seedlings.

After a week the survivors limped toward Petersburg
where my father's Confederate grandfather
was shot in the siege. And now this burial detail
of former slaves has been sent to do the work
the white men left undone.
All week they've gathered and dug.
Only one government issue boot is in any shape
to walk away. A balustrade

of ribs has collapsed inside a uniform.
The long ulna of an infantryman was dragged out
of its sleeve by crows or dogs.

I wish we'd kept driving that day,
following the muddy roads
until we found the family plot
with my great-grandfather's name chipped
in dark granite perhaps, his relations posted
around him like tent stakes. Winking
behind split-levels and furniture outlets,
the Chickahominy steered us into the woods
of the battlepark. Standing clear
of the crumbling breastworks,
the only tourists and all that quiet,
we spun the maps in our hands,
trying to make sense of the battlelines,
to picture so many dead so fast.

If I lie here long enough with the night's
last traffic brushing against the bed,
the crickets slowing to a throb,
will this man pull that knitted cap
from his head, wipe his face
and take up his shovel again? How does he reckon
the moons of calluses on his hands,
the clink of metal on bone?
The war is over, he's free, so he's heard.
How much can the golden scales rise
when he shovels the last mound, taps it down,
and brushes off his hands?
And when he goes on down the road,
a cornucopia curling through palmettos,
how much must he take with him?

We're no one he'd bother to imagine.
The face he lifts to the white photographer
is as black as he can make it.
We stood quiet in the quiet shade,
but we weren't quiet enough
to hear what he hears, blood drawn
into the spindly roots, into the saplings,
into the crowns above our heads,
and how the day comes on regardless.

Likeness

1. Extreme Unction

When Voltaire complained about the church
fathers making history with metaphor,
he was complaining about the likes of me
bringing sunlight into it, tiny keys
that spangle the prisoner in his cell
or Christ sliding across the water
like a braking pelican ...

But in his last hours what figures
played out in his head, what thin similes
that he called for the curate?
Outside the loose splash of a fountain
was too finite to bear, the leaf
sputter on the windowsill a word
too slight for ink and quill?
If you live for Truth, what's a little
unleavened bread, to hedge your bets?

And I can almost imagine it, admitting
at the end the well-groomed priest
to my bedside. He draws the damp sheet back
and oils my feet and hands, sprinkles me
like a shirt for ironing. But just the thought
of the host's papery taste revives

a thousand school day masses—the radiators
wheezing beneath the stations of the cross,
the nuns clicking us into genuflection:
Iamnotworthylamnotworthylam notworthy—

and metaphor lifts the shirt off the ironing board
and floats it through the window.
It folds its arms across its chest
and slips like a letter
into the slot between power lines,
flaps into the sky like the flag
of the spirit (never the spirit itself)
admitting some great reckoner
and shrinks and shrinks to a grain of salt.

Distilled from a test tube, they'd look
the same: blood salt, a dropper
of salt marsh, tears licked up secretly
by the hostage ("I'm still alive then")
or my two-year-old daughter ("I taste me").

2. In the Stairwell

I don't mean a basket of canaries sailed
by paper butterflies. And even the mundane
pickup truck has a *bed*
to carry kindling. Metaphor hitches the impossible
to the passable, the wonder
to the wanderer, tenor and vehicle.
The sun is a clarion and the wind in the cedars
angels choiring in our ears.

After the Christmas concert
I pulled at my friend Rosemarie's sleeve,
"I saw you. What was a good Marxist
like you doing singing along?"
And she smiling back, "And you, a good
atheist, all the words came back to you?"

3. The Golden Legend

Like all Catholic kids I prepared myself
early for martyrdom. I chanted the beatific
No's that St. Catherine broke the wheel with,
practiced the stubbornness of St. Denys
on Montmartre, denying his own death, refusing
to fall down where he was killed.
He picked up his severed head, rinsed it off
in a spring and carried it four miles
to the mountain he'd chosen
as his dropping place.
                                    In the garage
I would cut Rainbow bread with a milk glass,
flatten the moons into dry doubloons
that I dropped into my shirt
so my brothers, backyard Romans,
might shower me with the arrows we stripped
from the honeysuckle bush.

                              The best part was lying
with the cool mud against my back, blooming
like St. Sebastian (a bouquet of branches
shooting from each armpit) and never renouncing
though the soldiers poked me, their aluminum
helmets rattling on their heads like seed pods,
and the clouds made light of it all, inscrutable
grins that broke apart like toast and sped away.

So when I stopped believing, I didn't stop
admiring willfulness, great renunciations
that quench pyres, snap ax handles,
and change smuggled bread to roses.
Sunlight rains down keys so tiny they fit

in the tear duct, the fine spray sent up
as Jesus skids toward us like a pelican,
the bucket-beaked fisher of fish
that the old ones believed fed its young
by dripping its own blood down their throats.

4. De Kindermoord Te Bethlehem

It took crates of carrots and steady brushing
by strong-armed grooms to bring out
this lustre in the horses' coats. The gray knot
of cavalry and the lords sporting
Renaissance plumes do not dismount.
This is foot-soldier work. The work of halberd
and pike loose in ancient Judea, snow
on every rooftop. The anachronisms
remind us how little of history
is ever reeled in and put away. What happened

twines around *now* and *next*, a knot
in the garden hose that hisses and thrashes
across the lawn. None of these villagers
will shut this day up. They'll carry it
around like a wad of string
in their pockets, something to pick
and pick at: I forgive you nothing.
In the center of the canvas a woman
has sunk to the trampled snow, snow trampled
by hoof and boot. The peasants—their children
scooped up in their arms—are pursued
even into the picture frame. De kindermoord.
In Flemish the massacre sounds like kindling
snapping or small bones. There's no help

from above either—the sky is the same
squalid color as the snow, the yellow
residue of a grease fire. Her child's small
clothes stripped off and tossed beside her,
lost to the world, the woman rocks herself
above the appalling weight they've flung back
in her lap. Pale and pocked as a daylight moon.

Meanwhile, he's out of the picture,
the baby they were after. We will recognize him
in another gallery by the gold plate
fixed to his head. Smuggled south
where spring has already feathered out
the olive and the almond trees, he sucks
the meat of a peeled purple fig
held out in his mother's damp palm.

5. Experience

After his son died Emerson wandered
his essays trying to feel something again,
hoping that suffering might be it,
the nubbin of truth
that wouldn't melt on the tongue, but:
"The only thing grief has taught me
is to know how shallow it is." A puddle,
a pond, a creek, a wide oblivious river,
sooner or later you hit bottom.

What's the use of metaphor if it can't make loss
fathomable, and the loss of loss:
a fathom is the measure of the arms
outstretched. How to fathom
the child he would never hold again.

And what's the use of history if it can't
make us a bridge to watch the muddle
of what happened ravel towards us, braids slipping
around the pilings that lift us
from the drink and rush
of stuff that hurries under and onward
into what will happen next,
and next. Progress, the love of progress,
and the love of Now We're Getting Somewhere.

We count up what we've learned—
the gouged shore, driftwood
dammed in the rapids, the slow eddies
further back, but the anodyne river
flows into the lake of sleep

and those who know history are
as doomed as anyone else

wading in the understory.
History is no good for figuring somebody
simply walking home one March
from a dawn tennis match.
The desert air cools the sweat
on his neck, and, let's say,
he can make out the smell of the sea
woven inside the smell of coffee and snow
sloughing off the peak of Qurnet es Sauda.
A dark Mercedes rounds the corner
and that's the last he sees of history
for seven years: "I have become a bandied name
that floats in a white place, cramped
and smooth, like a sparrow egg."

Here comes the flotsam of the flooded house:
stair parts, highchair, Christmas cards,
low boat of a locked bureau. Upstream
keys and silverware fall through clouds
of minnows and sink into the mud.

6. Tour from the Cell

"Duck your head here where the stairway
curls us into the blue that day begins with,
now step onto the sunsoaked street
(feel the hair on your arms rising, the heat
under your shoes). Cover your eyes a moment.
Do you smell garlic and cardamom
and raisins? Coffee? That luffing sound
is rice poured in a basket, polished

infinitesimal pearls. Behind the jalousie
my wife braids her hair. On her long brown
fingers let's give her amethysts set in silver.
The saffron taxis wait for us. Let's circle
the fountain in the plaza, twirling our keys
and blowing smoke rings at the clouds."

7. After Auden

Rocking on his heels, reading the literature,
smoking, the young poet ("tall, with straw-
yellow hair and light hazel eyes")
stood where we stood in Room 31. Another December,
"the cold streets tangled like old string,"
1938. That month after Kristallnacht
you could feel what was coming, the cobblestones
throbbing under your feet, the click
of bolts in locks, shudders. Children
forbidden to go skating peek out,
but only a bit of tank, a wheel, the chin
of an officer fits in the keyhole.
Wheels rattling stone and the sound of gorgeous
creaking leather, the butter of their boots.

For an hour we slumped in the ancient chaise,
the velvet nap balding under our arms,
and joked how *Icarus*—smaller, duller
than we'd supposed—had shrunk and faded
from too much washing in poetry.
Among the distant gliding sea birds,
cormorants and pelicans? (curve of wing
fine as eyelashes above the headlands)
we searched for the father who by now
would have glanced over his shoulder
and doubled back, opening and closing
his winged arms around the updrafts
before the fathoms blinked over his child
and slapped against the delicate ship.

And I remembered Bishop writing Lowell
that about suffering Auden was wrong:

"the ploughman and the people on the boat
will rush to see the falling boy any minute,
they always do, though maybe not to help."
The eastbound traffic slows and snarls
to count the westbound sirens, look long
at the skid marks, the crushed car, an arm
dangling from a stretcher. And the shepherds
would soonest tramp down the hillside
for the miraculous birth of a two-headed calf.

8. Gravensteen

Back home I'd been following the story
like bread crumbs into the woods—news flash,
special report. The pale men appeared
one by one, first in Damascus in a flashbulb
storm, then on the balcony at Wiesbaden,
another white bath of attention.
I didn't much believe all the talk
of global village, electronic Earth,
but there I was in Ghent, in that strange orange
rhombus of a Eurostyle room,
glued to CNN updates, like people
in Paducah and Palermo, waiting for the last
US hostage, Terry Anderson, to step
onto the hospital balcony. Seven years
out of history: he looked intact
except his wire rims were missing a temple piece.

But I had a duty to sightsee, so while my husband
gave his paper at the university,
I forced myself into the Christmas crowds
along the Veldstraat, buttoned my Blue Guide deep
in my pockets to disguise myself, and strode
toward Gravensteen, the reconstructed Castle
of the Counts, a gray pile in the frozen river Leie.

Off season, I was the only person nosing
around the dim chamber, my breath misting
the display cases, not that I could read
the Flemish placards anyway. Double doors
for a dollhouse?—some arched devices
that met at screws, tiny padlocks dangling
like earrings from one side.
Whatever was laid out under glass,

I thought I knew enough to appreciate
the fortitude of craft. Though the blacksmith
had long ago sunk to dust and chalk,
what glowed once on his anvil, what he forged
in the white heat and clang, iron on iron,
was unchanged, a legacy to drift
toward us through the centuries.

I made out a long cot in a corner,
wrought-iron letters on poles, cleavers,
chains and bracelets: what was this place?
I picked out a few English cognates—
finger, justice, state prisoner—
and found I'd been admiring
thumbscrew, branding iron, "coercive bed"
in The Museum of Judicial Objects.

What was I so suddenly afraid of?
Hospital-hospitality-hostage-host:
like the knowledge of good and evil,
our words are tangled up, our little
victories over oblivion. The great cloth hall
is black with soot. The bolts of silk
the merchants wrangled over
were soon ragged, then lint, then less
than dust—seedlings for clouds, the speck
you can't find in your tearing eye.
The figures on Penelope's tapestry,
the thread, and then the loom.
What's left is our metalwork—the iron age,
the bronze age, the ages of spearhead,
arrowhead, manacle and the executioner's sword
—as unchanged as we are.

9. Likeness

A crookneck squash, a skeleton key,
the chevron penciling
of a flown bird, these are all "horse"
to our daughter. And the moon
that says O O between the trees sleeps
on the kitchen table, escorted
by fork and spoon. As it came to each of us,
language comes to her first in resemblance
shimmering between things, trailing
clouds of glory and metaphor.
But the double-eyed happenstance
in our "moon" doesn't make it moonier
than the sidelong glance in "maan"
or the cup in "luna."

With the kindling shed by the silver
maple I spell out HORSE for her.
Horse, I say, and she plops on the H's
crosspiece and rides it into slivers.
But when we park the car, jump the ditch
and wade thistle and stinkweed
to a pasture fence, Anna freezes against me,
clinging to my legs as the chestnut mare—
a sudden brown ocean of glistening flesh—
snorts the grass from my hands,
grinds it between large yellow teeth, then reaches
its neck through the barbwire for more.

FROM

No Private Life

(1990)

The Gloss Avenue Ghost

Open a door or window upstairs, and downstairs
            papers drift to the floor.
Or a scarf hung on a doorknob fans its tassels
        as if to finger the air's disturbances.
This house always breathed like that—my wife called
            it sympathy, but I knew it
                    as a drafty house. The lady who lives
            here now wasn't wakened,
as I was, when her oldest boys inched up
            their window and shimmied down
                    where an auto, taillights glowing,
    rolled down the hill before its engine
            started up and took them away.
        I try to watch after them
                    as far as I can. The mother worries.
Nine children. The mother and her mother—just a shadow
                        mumbling. And two fat orange cats
            that sleep in the windowsills—east, mornings,
            west, afternoons—and one shivering
    bitch puppy, pregnant her first year,
        forgotten tonight outside.
                    She ran barking after the boys,
but not fast enough, limped back
            and settled herself into a pile of leaves
            swept in a porch corner.

        I was here first, but no matter.
I always did like the hours
                    after a party—the world
            hushed like now, candles
    putting themselves out in their own puddles,
                quiet like the night river, close in to shore.

On the floor maybe a handkerchief
dropped when a sweating girl
finally let herself go in the dance. Upstairs,
my wife asleep in the nursery, the nurse
asleep in a chair.
This lady falls asleep
sitting up too, sometimes sleeps here
through the night, curling in
as it gets colder, until at dawn
she stomps her feet to wake them.
They hurt her like ungrateful children.
Now and then she'll start up and look straight through me
and around the room for balance
at the jackets and shoes with tongues loose
and newspapers, some twisted
into kindling then left
to unwind through the night,
or, one of her children comes down and shakes her
and pulls her arms.
We leave each other be—too many boats
in the middle of the river, too many
children in this house, three to a room
like cousins on holidays,
but these scramble against each other—
crabs in a bucket.
If you pilot the barges close along the banks
where the trees droop like velvet
to a theatre box,
and if you've lived with the river, like a wife or a house—
the wide shallow bends and sandbars
rising in the seasons—
you'll stay clear of the rest and wakeful
in courting the small danger. It floats

on the tongue like the last transparent
sliver of a lozenge.
My wife kept a bowl
of lemon drops like these and my head in her lap.
Lifting the sour sweet
past my lips, she talked me into more
than she ought, then let me drift off.

No one ever stays put in this house.
One now at the head of the stairs,
head cocked, squinting and hearing
a nervous leaf in the windy sills.
The crowding makes some of them mopey. Yesterday
I found one little girl squeezed
in the old coal chute with a novel
and a flashlight.
She put both down suddenly
and cried for a solid hour. And me there useless—
a stranger at a small-town funeral.
With my wife it was different.
Her sadness grew on her
like wild grapes. The vines can climb
from nowhere and up a river sycamore,
and the wide leaves spin
a twilight in a summer noon.
Nothing pleased her then.
Twice a day, she dragged
the furniture around as though some secret
clock signaled her.
Late into the quiet
sometimes, I hear the echoes of the bureaus
and wardrobes and divans scraping the floors,
years of drifting until a cliff face
caught the sound

and sent it home. All sounds float back
sooner or later though no one hears
        or they arrive without warning.
                The time I found her grasping
            against the bookcase, a trail of books
        spilling open as if trying to find a word
                for her, she had pried
            all the ivories from the piano
                    and dropped them
    in the commode.
            Her mother's piano,
all that was left of England.
                        She scared the daylights
            out of the girls. When I finally came home,
    riding up, they flew to me,
            pressed their faces against
                the haunches of the horse—
I had grown so large in my absence.
            But not large enough
    for them to remember—or want to—
                how they came running. These children
        are bad mannered,
            but they don't pretend to forget.

Too many boats in the middle, and too many
            children riding this house, a boat
    so low in the water, the river
            laps in.
That load of goosedown from Illinois—
                    it was not
        the sailing in close
                (despite the lawyers),
                    it was our damned, worthless

French boat—cracked in two.
A blizzard in July.
That lazy flatboater (lawyer's nephew) following us
for a river guide
nearly drowned
with feathers when he opened his mouth to curse us.
What's that dog
going on about now? Maybe the boys
coming home or someone sleepless
on Ridge Road.
Pitiful thing—
shaking on the step, barking
with bits of leaf stuck to her.
The trees along the river
grew feathers
as though leaves were a momentary disguise
and one by one each tree
would take wing
from the shattered boat
and barges riding
up the sandbar,
one on top the next,
the other boats spinning
around and over to avoid us.

One of the girls is running to shush the dog.
Barefoot on the porch,
a night like this. Muddy paw prints
up her nightgown.
My Nellie's age when they took her.
And is she carrying that little dog,
leaves and all, to bed with her?
If only all trouble could be soothed
with an embrace until you slept

under the weight of the wool.
She didn't get the door
                    shut tight. The grandmother,
        hunches over here, door wide open,
            dead of winter, calling the cats—
    which are sleeping upstairs.
        The girls hurry by as if they live
                    down the block.
Three days on trains
            to see my girls in Grand Haven
and they just stood on the stoop, grimly
                blinking to show no intention
                of asking me in.
It was after the wreck
    and the lawyers
                    she took them, that nothing
        brother of hers insisting.
            Bess was fat
        in all the wrong places. And Nell
    chewed her lip like a sentence
        in German till my eyes stung.
I should have shaken the silliness from them.
                They weren't mine anymore.
    I was no one but the house's
            which is only a house after all.
But then.
                When I'd be down to Memphis or Louisville
                and they still here, I'd lie awake
on my bed on the river—rocking above me
        the lantern on a hook, in good weather
            its handle clicking, a steady heart,
and I'd make the house up, pacing
                the rooms in my head—

the smell of turpentine
in the cellar cupboard, the "Morning
Gloriouses," as we called them,
climbing the screens. Nellie
hopscotching up and down, down
and up the stairs, bouncing twice
for the music
on the third last stair that always wheezed.
And then I wasn't on the river
but with them because longing
carries you home. She told me
some nights maybe she felt me here.
Maybe she did.

The lady's stretching awake now, complaining softly
over her stiff hands.
Reaching into the cushions, frowning,
she pulls out the blue ceramic horse
I saw the children bury solemnly last evening.
The ugly chair will keep her shape
a little while , then give it up
to the slow steady dawn. Holding herself
carefully in half-sleep, she'll look over each bed,
then for a few hours
lie on top her own.
The boys are back now
and almost all of us are asleep.

The Night of the Breaking Glass

A windshield crazy with breaks
like a skating rink deserted. The young
run random in the street. Upstairs, their families.
The drawn shades throb with the lights
from a squad car burning quietly below.
The cops hustle by in pairs,
wide-eyed, jangling with equipment. Invisible
as a loose page blown against door frames and worried
about the road, my father, the newsman, reels
into the summer of 1967, the race riot.
He's either drunk
or out of his mind—that delicate organ
misfiring, a gun carried
in the hat. He could find *the story of his life*
among the shards and blackened TV sets
and relay lines passing hand to hand
the wealth of a state store. He lived here once,
maybe that's why he shows up on this street
stumbling. He's lost his childhood
or found it
when he falls into the park, into the custody
of a juniper that keeps him,
as I would, for the night.

The moment a window shatters it looks like a pond
stirred up by a wishing coin
or a dropped body. And the faces,
losing their reflections in the rocking water,
could be breaking in grief
or in laughter. The viewer chooses
since the facts are indifferent.

When we make stories out of appearances
we almost control the world
that always controls us. The bicycle rusting
in the city dump, its one wheel
spinning with the breeze, we squint
until it's a baby's mobile. Or a cattle car
speeding into Poland.

Kristallnacht, 1938, an old Jew behind the curtains
looks down the street to the riot.
His shop will go soon, bricks raining
the glass across the checkered floor,
knocking over bolts of chenille and jersey,
he thinks, like wooden soldiers. The flames will race
up the sheer marquisette
he draped along the counter as down a road
that never ends since he never began it.
Shoe buckles will melt into black felt, going soft
like faces in old lithographs: with the jawbone
of an ass Samson scattered the Philistines.
But the old man reaches for his own face,
feeling for the bones that rise
more each year—the stones of a dying stream
whose town empties so quickly.

By the time they round the corner, he's changed
the brown shirts into loosed dam water
bobbing with torches. And he's prepared
for each glass bead that dissolves
like the sledding snows of his childhood.

My father rouses himself, hat in the grass, one leg
looped over a branch
as if it belonged to someone else.

Whatever story he made, to explain himself
to himself, out of the park trash
and his coat sleeve—torn off and folded
into his breast pocket—
he couldn't tell his children
since he didn't know where he'd been
and the tale reached us
with another meaning entirely.

FROM

Indian Summer

(1980)

Indian Summer

1

Sycamore, maple, beech thinning out,
but the earth's still soft: fingers
blotted with it
poke flower bulbs down—the last planting.
We do little work.
Streets full of traffic,
everyone's going somewhere
as if to put a last dollar on a horse.
This weather is a chance for something
to happen one last time.
People try marriage again,
someone falls in love,
an old woman, wrapped in her sweater,
looks out at the sky like an answered prayer.
Indian summer can last two days
or two weeks, and like any other day,
we'll die tomorrow,
but here's this wind, leaves
bright enough to bloom,
even the birds, uncertain, circle
in one wave and return to the branch.

2

After knocking again,
I cup my hands to the screen door to see in,
two flies circling over supper dishes,
milk left out.
Then I hear it—the brute swallow of air,
sobbing into a hand: *why don't you stop?*
In front the door slams,
taking the air with it.
I jump down the steps, splash through marigolds
and gray tomato leaves. A car starts up,
leaves leap up the street after it.
Holding my short breath in,
I let my back door slam after me.
My mother's quick look expects my father.
I go out, grab a rake from the leaves
and try to scrape the earth clean.

3

The axe splits the bright center of the red oak,
silencing the crickets.
Porches yawn with wood.
Still this warm wind, blowing all day through windows
open wide again,
will not let us believe in winter.
My sister and I, sweaters tied to our waists,
socks slipping in our shoes,
bounced our books into the leaves.
Waist-high we piled them—yellow maple, red sweetgum, oak
soft as leather—then climbed in
until we sank in the fragile odor of leaves.
We pulled stems through our braids
and hummed the Indian
sounds we knew: *iroquois, cherokee,*
ohio, miami, cree,
spread out under the endless sky of this weather.

4

From their mothers' gardens in spring,
some bring tulips and daffodils,
lilacs heavy and wet as grapes. Only old roses,
the last family left, grow in our yard,
so my mother makes the May altar for the Virgin,
carves gothic doors from an old box
and paints it blue. But in fall
papery maple leaves are nothing
to bring. I close my eyes
and walk home through them. My fingers search
the air for the surprise
of tree trunk or low branch.
This is what it is like to move in a slow circle of sound,
hear leaves *wissh, wissh* their deep muddy smells.
Sunlight red apples through my squeezed lids.
When I open them, I've wandered against a stone.
I look up and down the bright new street,
hiding the secret—it's like the movies
where the girl with amnesia
touches the grainy bricks of a house
and is finally home.

Low Moon

5

I am fifteen and the boy,
whose jokes I've listened to for two weeks,
takes my wrist and leads me from the party,
away from houses new in corn fields.
He lifts me over a fence, his hands finding
the right places. We climb up to a pasture.
My breasts, still strange to me, find their own way.
Side by side in grass cows mumbled over in summer,
we watch house lights go out below,
big dipper rising in the veins of trees.
I weave loose blades through my fingers
until he leans me back.
Years later the smell of leaves reminds me
of that warm wind
rising inside me, how all that night
I press my body against my bed,
float in and out of sleep,
remembering how his hand stopped
along my sweater and my breast pushed toward it
before I pulled away his fingers
and we walked back toward the low moon.

6

In spring, wind left from winter. In fall,
this warm wind gathered far off.
It sent milkweed feathers from our sticky hands,
caught here and there in the brown grass.
My father sang us dry between towels
and it spread the song
so all the neighborhood could hear.
My mother called as I straddled thin limbs.
Wind rocked me in that bed of branches and leaves.
Over the logs it whistled
on the dark porch, flapped my sweater
open against the boy's arm.
Now nothing hides from us.
Through the gleaning trees, brighter than any northern sun,
we begin to see again—
houses along the ridge appear, almost shyly, windows
burn all afternoon. Old voices
of leaves say what I can't
as your hands start the wind in my hair.

7

Father staggers up the trellis.
We crouch at mother's bedroom window.
The curtains breathe.
Streetlight streaks my hair
as I braid and unbraid it.
My older brothers and I sneak looks at mother.
She searches the dark for our faces,
for something we can't tell her.
Father lies on the porch roof, whispering her name.
I watch the small slur of his cigarette,
he's vague as fallen branches, leaves
spilling over the rain gutters.
We speak in low voices
of late-night radio that glows by the bed.
One brother slides along the carpet to the door;
the house is quiet
except for his dialing the phone.
In the distance the hollow sound of a car fades.
Then the flashlight, the police
calling father by name.
A light next door goes on, off.
He shrugs a few curses and climbs down to them,
disappearing over the eaves into the gray light
breaking above every house in the neighborhood.

Rain

8

Nothing could live under our feet.
Summers we ran the grass brown;
by fall it was mud.
I stand barefoot on the dirt for its smooth feel.
Squinting against the sun,
my mother hardly sees me
as she carries the ninth baby up the walk.
Shoes click on the pavement.
Spreading stars of dandelions
overflow the cracks.
She says, "see" and opens the blanket carefully.
The new one's black hair sticks out,
her eyes big as coins.
The red hand with the hospital bracelet
grabs at light or at wind.
Oak leaves swing in the trees.
I knot the hem of my dress against my legs.
It sounds like rain.

9

Sundays at the zoo he roars at them,
they pace the cages and roar back—
no need to tell your mother ...
The lamp shades sway,
on the mantelpiece photographs jump.
We play lions.
Father growls across the carpet, claws the air
with his fingers. One by one
he snatches us, hugs us to his wet shirt.
Circling him like Indians,
we close in on the smell of gin and pile on
until he gives into the floor.
One eye open, he groans
beneath the happy heap of our bodies.

10

My bony knees crease with dark Ohio dirt.
My brother and I shovel through mud and roots to clay.
A thousand years an inch, his teacher says.
If we had skimmed off only the fine grains
that cling to my hand when I lay it flat,
and pressed our ears a breath-deep
below the surface, maybe we could hear his voice.
The handles of the spades shine
beneath our hands. We dig farther
than anyone remembers.
When the metal clinks we are ready
for anything but the blunt rock we lug out.
The late sun shatters it
into hundreds of crystals a second.

11

A friend tells me how a man, lungs fillings with dust,
plastered a fortune
in his bedroom wall and died.
Years later the city took the house for taxes.
The neighborhood kids were there
when the wrecking ball, trailing the powder
a house ends in, broke through.
Twenties and fifties swirled out like startled birds.
I want to think that old man planned it—
soft bills fluttering over the Baptist church,
over the fruit stands at Ray's grocery,
into the quick hands
of children who have everything
to spend it on.

12

We shake off leaves sticking to our feet.
My sister fumbles with her keys
and the bottle of wine
breaks as messily as her marriage will.
I grab her son from the shards,
he likes the sound of glass.
We know the stories so well—
her husband wants her to be patient,
the man I live with wants a woman
like wind. When I touch him
his eyes are quick stones. Even in sleep
he keeps his breath close.
Voices drift down the block—
kids joking under streetlights, one leg swung
over the bicycle in perfect balance.
Mornings I leave him the dark bedroom.
I stretch out on the warm carpet and the sun,
climbing through new spaces in trees,
floats through me until I hear
cars on the road out of that city.

Peacock

13

I go slow enough so
the peacock, dragging its tail like an old blanket,
follows me down the paths of the zoo,
the only safe place to walk in the neighborhood.
From the elephant house I see my windows
where the man I live with is sleeping still.
When I hold him his body is frail as a girl's, thin
as the plants he eats.
Only a few walk here—high school boys
tapping at the glass before fruit bats, an old woman
sprinkling corn to pigeons,
and a couple hiding against an oak.
At their feet leaves shine
like his leather jacket she crushes at the shoulder.
This peacock knows I'm flattered.
He keeps his distance, like a cat, and the lions,
leopards, cheetahs, jaguars, white Bengals—
famous here—are out in the early air.
They've padded a path along the fences;
it circles always back
to the mounds of meat buzzing in the tins,
where the lioness, that perfect hunter,
her coat the color of late grass,
practices at thin air.

14

In the tumble of sheets
and broken shadows of fading trees,
we float back. The world suddenly
quiet. And through the screen door, the wind,
heavy with the scent of drying, comes to us.
I am all I remember.
This wind carries moments
the way a passing car threads us with a dim song
we heard once in someone else's arms.
In each memory, I am
voiceless as the dead—my smaller self leans
before my mother mumbling in her sleep
about the mortgage. I cannot tell her that money
will come but not a man, that the azalea
she saved for dies in next winter's ice.
I cannot describe to another the rain,
the truck—how to stay alive.
Even now, listening with you to pure last light,
the body memorizing the curves of our hands,
the woman I will be remembers
when a window sparks with sun
and she closes her eyes to let this wind take her.

Uncollected Poems

Fentress Creek

When the neighbors have nursed their nerves
on enough Strawberry Ripple,
they stumble down Polk Street towards Mama's
and nudge me, Hey what'd you think about
while you was shooting him?
And I could spit. Thinking.
With that guy, pants bunched around his knees,
stinking and speckled with whatever
lunch he had. Not to mention
his eyes scrunched up, slobbery lips.
And oh, oh, he'll learn me a thing or two.
Think about. Take a little pause
like for a smoke? Consider
the pull on the trigger, the bird squeak
in the trees, the creek
stammering past the campsite? Shit.
Once I get ahold of that gun, I shoot him quick
as I can, scramble out that tent, and I'm gone.
I don't look back at what he looks like
except the way you do on the highway—
just let the wreck glide off your eyes,
turn the radio way, way up,
no matter what song. Takes too much effort
to boo the neighbors off Mama's porch.
They plug the bottlenecks with their thumbs,
fidget on the stoop, all the while
trying to figure a way—like counting money
they don't have, won't ever have—
to get me talking about it.
Like I took polaroids of him and the sticky
sleeping bag. Once I'm loose,
it's only, Where the fuck am I?

But I'm already running. Where my shoes
went to who knows. He took them
straight off, first night.
So my feet are bleeding too—
roots and prickers and rocks I don't feel—
when I find that store and, Don't you dare
come in here like that, Girl.
But I walk on in like I own the place.
A sort-of walk, a sort-of limp
since it's sore. I grab me a pack of Salems,
rip the wrapper from a Bic lighter,
saying, Call the cops. The flame
leaps a mile high about, shriveling up
my bangs. That's when my hands
jump around like I can't stop them.
I just killed a piece
of shit in the woods, call the cops.
Over and over. Wet cold coke. Sit in a chair.
The doofus deputy knows it all,
though he has to read questions
off a special sheet, keeps poking at
his crackling radio, ten-four.
That's bad for your health, he tells me
about Salems, Stunt your growth.
Gee whiz, kindly fuck yourself—
but I don't say it. Three weeks,
all I have to eat is Jewelette Donuts,
creek water from a bucket and some pizza
left in his truck once. Night and day dancing
to a tree except when, I'm gonna
let you out your bracelets now.
And him unhitching his belt
like he's Christmas. I'm a jawbreaker

when he comes at me: crack his teeth
if he tries to crack me, slipping
off my pink layer, slipping off my purple,
shrinking like eyes under bright lights.
Another day and I'd be down to the powder,
the grain on the tongue that gets away whole.
So I blink and blow the smoke
in Smokey's face, Excuse me, I say,
real sorry about that. And I'm swearing
if he leaves me alone one second
in the cruiser I'll peel out of there—
I bet I could've drove it—gravel flying
like hard clouds, laying tar,
lights and sirens all the way to Mama's,
and her running out, hands flapping
by her head like extra ears, Oh my baby,
Oh my baby—like she did that first time
I run off. Seems just like yesterday
though not even yesterday is yesterday.

The Enchantment

Where was I meaning to go?
That smooth dirt under my bare feet under the branches
was like walking on shiny palms
of old people. I had parted the thicket—
which ran between the houses like the shock of hair
down an animal's back—enough
to see the old woman, half-lying
on the back porch, rocking in her arms
her middle-aged retarded son.

Front porch a screen of trumpet creepers, the house
we crossed down the block to avoid.
Rising from the hill, its two gables—
shades partly drawn—stared down
with weariness or threats, depending on the light.
The house of the child who never grew up.

But the backyard was open as a plate,
a plate of flowers I'd not seen before.
Beneath a purple-leaved tree, rode a stagecoach
birdbath. Two sparrows showered the water
down their wings and splashed
the garden path. The couple
on the steps stopped rocking.

He reached a posy of clover from the steps
and dragged it over her frizzy hair.
The world did not lean over, as in holy cards,
centering then beneath stricken trees and a cloud
of angels tensing like dragonflies.
Though she did cup his face and look steadily
as Giotto's Mary into the moment. Then it started—
a sound like sobbing but with something in it

I still have no language for.
She shifted her weight and drew him in again.
Or did he press his head against her slight chest,
his eyes white as he listened
for a common heart?
                    I felt horses
pounding up the path that shot out
from their feet and through the flower beds,
winding darkly under the birds, flying
under the weeder, its claw scratching the air,
and stopped where I stood shivering.
For he'd turned his face towards me
and I'd walked out of the cover of the trees.

Falling Into Place

I hear a creek running its banks—
the sound of wind freed in branches.
Dirt draws a net across my hands.
Burrs ride my coat.

I had to cross a railroad bridge,
watching water glide under my small steps,
had to pull myself up each slope
with thick vines to get up here.

Oaks have pushed off what's left of winter.
Earthworms move through new soil beneath leaves.
Below wide wings of trees we hid from hikers—
he spread his shirt out and we heard one breath.

He lifted the grass from my hair blade by blade.
I told him of the still place inside,
the sound of his name at night.

———

In spring, houses recede into the privacy of leaves.
He entered the green air to his house.
We spoke in translation.
He pressed one hand to my thigh, the other circled
my waist, measuring the space we never closed.

I pulled him against me and his voice hid deep in his body.
His weight pushed down on me. My body braced
for the fall into heaviness,
but I drifted off.

If I had looked out, I might have seen the Milky Way,
shimmering eggs of light. I dove into it once, naked,

from a boat. Water warm as my body,
I could have stayed under for hours.
Coming up, houses lit up the distance.

I curved my body into him each night
the way the water opens over sand.
Light edged the curtain.

———•———

Once he framed me in a photograph,
exposed where my body ends,
space begins. In the background lay the beach
strewn with winter wreckage, forgotten storm
fence sagging
in the same curve of one strand of my hair.

I picked shells into the pocket I made of my shirt,
slid my finger along the smooth
underside of a surf clam, poured water
from a moon shell, held it around in my hand.
He snapped the shutter.

We argued that day.
Maybe clouds blowing off the sea
pressed him too hard, splintered the sun,
or a stray dog pulling sticks from the water
gave him sadness.

———•———

Now I try to read lines where the water rose
and these oaks stood listening for fish.
I walk through these trees easily,
in a few weeks they will sew themselves together.

Under low limbs of spruce pinecones sink.
Each scale, sticky with sap,
readies to root beneath needles thick as a bed.
On the way home I hear the earth—
pale buds unfolding to the wind,
rain falling into place.

Some Will Tell You

It's light flung from your mother's scarf
(onto dad's old Plymouth, that pilgrimage),
thousands of silk top hats and gloves though
these days whoever wears...
wearing thin as the sound of a lawnmower
of childhood, the lawn torn into patches
small as dimes, or lightning bugs,
all the king's men couldn't stitch back.

It's the luffing sails of a marriage
gone the way of twin beds
and never the twain. On the night stand
the minute hand eating the pie away.
Where is she, is he tonight
when the moon hooks its empty bowl
and would lower it, like love, or the hood
of invisibility, over our heads?

It's finding the man who lost his hat
or his wife which was his hat. You could
read a book about it. The creatures
in his head somehow took a wrong turn—
the Arctic sunset, thick as sherbet,
he tells you, meaning sweet and festive,
and the way the tongue slides
on it... positively Ciceronian.

It's a matter of medieval saints
rubbing up against the furniture
of philosophy. You can't lift your chin
for the pearly headdress. And plenty
of quills, and pungent droppings. Sniff the velum
with the wiley Thomists and their angels

are all buttoned-up, wings like, like . . .
(but that's the point, pinpoint, the head
of a pin) . . . the fringed sleeves
of a country western star?

Or how it rained ever since,
say, Philadelphia. Coast to coast.
The mountains sliding us like plates
across their shoulders. It was a road
that went nowhere until we went there,
stretched our legs and breathed in.
The ruffed spirits of trees along the old
ski trail leaned against our heads
and took every last breath.

Interviews
1996-2017

with *New Letters on the Air* host
Angela Elam

Michelle Boisseau served as associate editor of BkMk Press from 1995-2017. *New Letters on the Air*, a nationally syndicated radio program about writers and writing since 1977 and affiliated with *New Letters* magazine and BkMk Press, featured Michelle as a guest several times. Below are excerpts from these interviews in which she reflects on her work. The 2017 interview was conducted before a live audience at the Kansas City Public Library.

October 30, 1996

ANGELA ELAM: I'm always looking for the person behind the words, and I could see you, but I was also surprised somehow, knowing you and what a straightforward person you are. There are so many layers going on in your language. It takes a lot more studying of the poem than it does of who you are as a personality, because you are what you present, or you seem to be anyway, and your poetry is so multi-layered.

MICHELLE BOISSEAU: Well, I think that's one of the things that often draws us to poetry. We get someone who takes us by the shirt collar, as Whitman does, and we have this voice, this self, that just pours himself, herself, itself, out of the page toward us. But I think there's another element of poems, and some of my favorite poets are those poets whose works are like paintings. The more you look at them, the more features you see in them. And that's what I try to do. I think maybe sometimes my poems get overbuilt. I like to imagine that when I'm putting a poem together, when I'm thinking about it, working on it, that I try to find out for myself what the etymology of any word is, for example, that I'm interested in using. And why it's there, and how that might be an avenue for another place to inspect in a poem. I think the more interstices there are in a poem, the more the poem will hold together. It is a created object, it's a created thing, but it's not a thing that can be destroyed very easily. Pulling one thread out will—it will still adhere. There's more to pick, so to speak.

AE: Well, this book, *Understory,* how long have you been working on it?

MB: Well, one of the poems goes back to before I finished my first book. But it didn't fit in that book. "The Pink Swing." Which is about my stepdaughter. I think I started working on that in 1988.

AE: Molly Peacock, who was the final judge for the Morse Prize with Northeastern University, was really taken by the imagery in that one and by the way you handle family life in your poetry. You deal with being a mother and being a stepmother, but in a very unsentimental way. You're very honest about the pain that comes in this sort of modern-day family.

MB: Motherhood gets sentimentalized a lot, but if you remove yourself and imagine yourself to be an anthropologist in your own life, which is, I think, what artists often do—just sort of step back and ask: What does this mean? What does this signify? What is this suggesting? One of the excitements about being a parent or being involved in any relationship is that you participate in a grand drama that people have always participated in. And you come to understand that you behave in a way that you hadn't anticipated you would when it was all much more theoretical. You know, that old axiom that you become your mother, you become your parents.

Something else is that being on the other side of childhood, being the parent and having a child, seeing that child grow, develop, become a person—you also see a person becoming a human being. We don't start human. We become human. It's really magnificent. To be sentimental about it is to be untrue. Because it's more magnificent than this sentimentality of these kids with big eyes and puppy dogs and all that. There's something hard and true and authentic that needs to be acknowledged. Keats says, in one of his letters, that if poetry doesn't come as easily as leaves to a tree, maybe it shouldn't come at all—something like that. And I thought about that, and I often think, it's not easy for me. I'm not really a poet. It doesn't come as easily as leaves. And I thought, I don't know . . . do leaves come so easily to trees? Isn't there an incredible drama of those leaves unfurling themselves. They come naturally, but each leaf is a struggle. Walking is a natural occurrence for children, but it's really complicated. So is the acquisition of language, so is the acquisition of the soul, whatever that might be.

AE: You've called this book *Understory*. What comes to mind, of course, are the smaller shrubs and bushes that are underneath the large trees in the forest. What made you pick this as the title of this collection?

MB: It seemed to carry the freight of a lot of different issues I was dealing with. Part of the setting of this book comes from where I was when I wrote most of it, which was in Eastern Kentucky. We lived in a hollow, so we were surrounded by trees all the time. And at times, in July or August, there would be a sense that the green of the world was just too much. Robert Frost has the sense that nature will find its way and will triumph, ultimately, and nature includes all kinds of things like mortality. The understory is what the next generation is, what will come up. Sometimes it will, and sometimes it won't.

It's also the stuff that you ignore because it's not so glorious. It's the stuff that's in the way, that impedes your entrance into the forest. The woods being that place in which we're confused about who we are and where we're going. And we go into the woods, and we try to find our way out. And even when we think of history . . . In a sense, we go into history trying to find out who we are, where we are, and we get lost in it. Partly because of the understory. That image, that word just kept coming up.

Also, there's the story under the story. The story under the story is underneath our everyday actions, the way we behave—the story underneath that. Are we the individual stories under the larger story of humanity, or is the larger story of humanity underneath us?

AE: The book has three parts.: the first part is more personal about your family, and then the second part branches out a bit more. The third part was the most complicated section of the book because there's one poem, *Likeness*, that has nine different sections. Can you talk about it a little bit?

MB: Likeness in itself is the ultimate—is the fundamental way by which we know. When children begin to learn language, one of the first ways they learn it is through likeness. For example, a child, if they know the word for a plate, and they don't know the word for moon, will call the moon a plate. And that, of course is metaphor. When languages got created in this prehistory of whoever we are, part of it came out of that kind of association. We know all kinds of words that have connections to what they look like or what they sound like.

AE: You deal with that in the poem because you're talking about hostages. You begin to explore different words that have the same roots.

MB: We have the word *host*, which has this wonderfully warm sense of generosity. We also have the word *hostage*, which has a similar root. *Hospital* comes from the same root. Even *hotel* comes from that same root. Now all of these together, they have the same parents, but they go off— one is Cain, one is Abel—they go off in their various ways. But when we think, we use language. We are pulling together. It tells us these things are connected to each other. *Host* and *hostage* are connected to each other. It tells us something about who we are. What human endeavor does. Our capacity for good and evil, for example.

That poem that you're referring to is about Terry Anderson, partly. I was in France and Belgium with my husband. I had been obsessed with when the American hostages began to come out of Lebanon, where Terry Anderson had been for seven years. Seven years of bad luck—there's imagery of the mirror in there. I was trying to play with that notion. I was thinking of what it would be like—those seven years meant everything to me as an adult. My whole life changed from one of dark confusion into great happiness. And Terry Anderson missed all that. I was fascinated with him. So, I was very much paying attention to the story. The day he was released, I was sitting in this hotel room, waiting for him to come out. I was thinking what a bizarre thing—I didn't know who he was, but I had this incredible interest in him, wanting to see if he was OK. Then I walked out—I said, I can't just sit in a hotel room watching the news all day. This is silly. I'm in Belgium. I should be out exploring. Communing, rubbing elbows with the Belgians. I think that was what inspired it, all those different things. I was trying to explore the effect of the day on me. I think, as a matter of fact, the whole poem grew out of that moment and things that happened on that day. That reference to Brueghel—Belgium is where a lot of those paintings were created and where a lot of them are. "Musée des Beaux Arts," Auden's famous poem. The more I started thinking of all these different elements, it almost seemed to be getting sort of global. It started just by dropping one little pebble into the surface of this imagery. It radiated in many, many different directions and, of course, absorbed everything I was obsessed about, including my daughter and my husband, and growing up Catholic—every element seemed to be related. Part of the approach was, how is it related?

AE: Going back to the structure of this book, why three parts? What made you divide the book the way you did?

MB: Part of it was to start with the problem of language and how language answers and doesn't answer what we ask it to give us. To begin there and then to move back into the development of language, humanity, and self through the child. One of the problems that motherhood presents is your relationship to female history, the history of women. That issue is brought into the second section, as well as other issues about women's relationship to history. Exploring where consciousness is. How language works itself apart from this notion of childhood, and so on. Those poems gravitated around each other. Hopefully there's a passage—I knew where I wanted to start, and I knew where I wanted to end. The second section is kind of a tunnel that has many kinds of underground streams that will lead us into the notions that get explored in the last section.

Part of it is also to look at exploring some of the issues about female experience, to look at some things that are usually considered male experience, like the poem "Cold Harbour," about the Civil War. Of course, I have not fought in the Civil War; that's not reality to me. I feel a great deal of sympathy with people, not only in the infantry and fighting it, but the people who find the Civil War as a means of understanding who we are, where we began, or how we became the country that we are now. Is that denied to me because I'm a woman and I wouldn't have been able to fight in the Civil War? To isolate ourselves in terms of gender and any one particular kind of experience seems a very narrow approach. I think the imagination is often non-gendered.

March 12, 2007

AE: You're such a person of history. Anybody who reads your books can see how history plays a part in your seeing where we are today.

MB: I've always been a reader of history, just for fun, even when I was a kid. I've always been interested in how history gives us a sense of how to view our own place in our time, because we can always draw analogies from the past, one way or another. But, also, to see how, in a sense, un-special we are, how much we need to re-gard ourselves, our times, the people that we love, the people that we're charged to take care of, how we need to regard them as special, because history is indifferent. Only the individual, standing in the moment of time in which we can live, can make us care. I think what great historians do is to make us care about something that is seemingly very remote from us. They make us realize that, caring for that, maybe we can also expect others to care, who are not directly related to us, and then we can also be expected to care for others who are not directly related to us, either.

AE: And in a sense, that's what the poet does, too, don't you think? You tell these poignant stories within a poem that make the reader care about someone, whether it's an imaginary life or a life that was true to your own.

MB: Right. I think that happens in poetry. It happens in fiction, of course, all the time with historical fiction. But poetry is such a distillation of experience into almost one moment or a bringing together of multiple things. It doesn't have to concern itself with a lot of things that history may have to or that a narrative may have to in a novel where it's supposed to create a whole material world. Oftentimes a poem can engage us through just one phrase and hit us at a really fundamental level of what our humanity is about, which is directly connected to language, to voice, to the words that we use to create our own experience. A lot of linguists claim language is what makes us human. And it's that really intense relationship with language that we have through poetry that can connect us to ourselves.

January 11, 2010

AE: I want to talk about your most recent book of poems called *A Sunday in God Years*. There's part of an ad that you end up including in the book in the poem called "A Reckoning" ...

MB: In some ways, this ad propelled the book. My father died, and he had all these papers, and some of them were documents of family trees, which were sketchy; he didn't really have enough information. As I began to search online, this third cousin and I connected, and he had all this material. He sent it to me with this ad, and it so unsettled me that I had to—the only proper response for a poet is to think about it in terms of poems, because poetry is what drives you the deepest into thought. The ad, which offered a reward for a runaway slave named Gibson, was placed by my father's great grandfather in the *Richmond Enquirer* newspaper in 1834.

My dad didn't really know that much about that side of the family. I knew there had been these stories that my dad used to tell—that we had owned slaves and had money at one point and had lost it in the Civil War. So, I always kind of knew this, but I didn't really think about what that meant. I don't know if Gibson ever got away; I hope he did. But likely he didn't, or he didn't get far, or even if he did get away, to where? He had a hard life, wherever he ended up, and it would be another thirty-plus years until slavery was outlawed. It's so enormous. So much of the landscape that we think of, not just in the South, was built by forms of labor that are totally unjust, and we don't even see it anymore. So, part of this book is to start seeing it. Even simple things like the cotton gin, cotton production, the cotton mills in the North—none of this stuff is independent.

I kind of felt a repugnance in the writing process itself. Seamus Heaney talks about this in some regard about the troubles in Ireland; that you feel if you write a poem about it, aren't you using this horror, in a way, producing something out of it. There's a guilt you feel about it, and the poem itself becomes about that guilt. This kind of wrenching feeling: Is this appropriate? Can I talk about this? I showed the poet, fiction writer, and essayist Al Young an early version of the reckoning poem, a version ten years earlier, when I first tried it out. He pointed out the ad and said, I think you should start over here. I looked at the poem again—I wasn't hurt by it enough. You know, I hadn't troubled myself enough by it. I was at a distance, at an artistic distance from the material, and I had to get closer. I thought one of the things that I have to do is let Gibson talk. Of course, this is an imaginary Gibson, talking to me, as if he can talk to me from wherever he ended up.

The poem ended up trying to express . . . it's not a done thing. It can't be finished—it can only be a continuing process of reckoning.

March 23, 2017

AE: You have five books, and the one we're going to talk about tonight is *Among the Gorgons*. I've interviewed you before about your various books; it was fun to go back and listen to our first interview together, which was in 1996. It was so interesting to hear the programs and how you've grown as a poet. The emphasis in your life—the first time we talked, your daughter was five, maybe, and so motherhood was really at the forefront of what you were doing. Then, of course, *A Sunday in God-Years*, you're dealing so much with history, but also kind of the geologic history. And now we come to *Among the Gorgons*.

MB: The gorgons, the most famous one was Medusa, who has snakes for hair, and Perseus comes to kill her. I was thinking about that legend for a long time. I wrote to a friend of mine, who often deals with issues of mythology, and I said, I think the thing is that she didn't have snakes for hair, it was just that he was scared of her because she was old. I started thinking that after your kids grow up, you enter a different place. There's this group of other women who are saying "You know, we don't care anymore. You think we do? Nope."

AE: The gorgons—there were three, right? And two of them live forever…

MB: As we know from all of myth, immortality is a terrible curse. I was thinking about this recently in a conversation with some students. One of the subjects of all poetry, in a way, is the beauty of mortality, because it gives meaning to things. It's actually one of my aesthetics, that only with endings do we see the range of things. That's what makes anything poignant—that it's going to end.

AE: I was thinking about how you look at the aging of women through your books. It follows along with you aging and understanding the different times that you go through. You were employ-ing myth then, as well. It has been a theme for you.

MB: Myth and any kind of painting, sculpture, music, history—it's a vehicle to talk about certain kinds of feelings. It comes with its own apparatus of a story that's already built into it in a way that you can play off of, rather than having to build a whole backstory. Poems really work best when they work in an intense, immediate way. Although, I'm not going to argue against the epic, but the po-ems, especially as I get older, I'm more attracted to are the ones that you want to memorize, that you want to carry around, you want to have by heart. That has to happen in a small space. And if you already have this backstory...

AE: It's interesting that you're talking about poems you want to memorize. Are you still doing that?

MB: I can't stop doing that, in a way.

AE: What are you working on now?

MB: I have poems posted up around my desk that I pull down and look at. Also, I turn them around in my head, certain parts of them, all the time.

AE: I wonder, since you're in the process—once a poem takes hold of you, are those the poems that you then use? There are so many of your works where you have a line from another poet that you've built on. Is that the beginning of that process? Or does it work in different ways?

MB: I can't figure out exactly how it works. If I could... Every poem has its own autobiography, or biography, anyway. A phrase can start it, a sound—there's a certain kind of rhythm. I have a lot of poems in my head. I start hearing them, and then I think "Oh, this is the sort of thing where that sort of rhythm would work."

Recently, I was listening to a BBC broadcast of *Macbeth*, and I've been playing around with this line ... I don't know if it's going to stay in the poem. But one of the three weird sisters says, "I have a pilot's thumb." And the other one, she says, "I will drain him dry as hay." I put that down on the top of a page and started playing with that. I don't know how many times I've seen *Macbeth* and listened to it, read it, and all of a sudden that just jumped out at me. Sometimes it works that way.

AE: Tom Stroik (Michelle's husband) is a linguist. Tom's at the heart of a lot of queries into language. You guys have been talking about language for a long as you've been together, haven't you?

MB: That's how we fell in love, arguing over Sir Philip Sidney. He kept saying Sidney was this protestant messenger of Queen Elizabeth. I said, "That's ridiculous. He's a Petrarchan through and through." I was thinking aesthetics. He was thinking politics. We could probably start an argument about the same thing tonight.

AE: Your relationship with your mother was really ... Do you want to talk a little bit about that?

MB: I was the oldest daughter—she had nine kids in eleven and a half years. She was college educated, grew up in a middle-class household. Her mother worked, so she was raised partly by her grandmother. She married, converted to Catholicism, and started having all these babies. My father had a nervous breakdown when I was in third grade. Difficult things happened, and my mother went back to work. It was hard.

She was a very brave woman. She would drive anywhere, go anywhere; she'd try anything. She'd say, "Get in the car. Let's just— let's just go." I'd say, "What if we get lost?" She'd say, "You can't get lost. You always end up somewhere. You're always going to be somewhere. We'll find out—let's find out where this road goes." She wanted us to see something special.

AE: I was trying to think, "What are some things we've never talked about?" One of them is that you've worked a lot helping edit certain books of poetry. I wanted you to talk a little about being a literary citizen, because I see editing as being a literary citizen.

MB: Part of it's the textbook *Writing Poems*. When Robert Wallace first brought me into working on the fourth edition of *Writing Poems*, I was reluctant to do it. I ended up doing five editions. When I was hired at the University of Missouri-Kansas City, I was asked if I wanted to work as an editor at BkMk Press. One of the first books I edited was Alice Friman's *Inverted Fire*.

Through the different books that I've worked with—it's like helping the person realize their vision. I may ask, "Why is this line working like this? Because it seems like it's saying this, when I think you mean it to say this." So, then the author can, as I used to say to my students, have the excruciating pleasure of going back through a poem and trying to make sure that there's nothing jiggly or soft. Really tighten it up. It's hard for a poet to get a distance from the work, to understand, "what is the central nexus of this book?"

Sometimes they organize the book in a negligible way that doesn't put as much power into it. I also try to say, maybe this isn't the best poem—you don't want to have this poem in the book. I do that with myself all the time. There's lots of stuff on the cutting-room floor. Poems that have been published in important places don't end up in the book because they bring up something that's irrelevant or some other poem does better. They're just taking up space. Every poem demands a certain kind of attention. If another poem gets the attention better, and the other one's just making noise in the background, then clear the space so the other one has a bigger hall to sing in.

AUDIENCE QUESTION: When did you decide that being a poet was something that you wanted and that it was going to be part of the definition of you?

MB: As an American, you feel like an idiot going around saying "I'm a poet." It's like saying, "I'm an acrobat." I loved history; I loved philosophical issues, and I remember some of the nuns, when I was a senior in high school, reading "Intimations of Immortality." I thought it was so amazing.

A couple of other times I had written something, and someone said I should make it into a poem. By that time, when I was a senior, I was trying to write poems, partly because I was so bad at typing, and I could make poems in a much smaller area. I was drawn to language. I remember that I was going around quoting, "Blow, blow thou winter wind. Thou are not so—" I loved the sound and loved playing around with it. That was part of it. It took a long time because I was such a bad poet. When you start writing poetry, you're pretty bad, so you might just say, "I'm a writer." After a while, when you publish enough, you can sort of say, "Yeah, I'm a poet." But usually you wouldn't admit it.

But everybody's a poet, in a sense. It's a natural instinct to take your language and play around with it. I think it's so discouraged— anything that's aesthetic or tries to be. If you do something that doesn't make money in our culture, it seems ludicrous. But it's that passion. In a lot of ways our education discourages the natural inclination to art, music. Shuts it down like it's not practical, when it's really the most practical thing in the world—to use our minds way outside of its limitations.

BIOGRAPHY

Michelle Boisseau was the author of several previous books of poetry, including *Trembling Air*, a PEN USA finalist, *Understory*, winner of the Morse Prize, and her university textbook, *Writing Poems*, initiated by the late Robert Wallace and co-edited most recently with her colleague Hadara Bar-Nadav. Boisseau was a Guggenheim fellow and received two fellowships from the National Endowment for the Arts. Prior to her untimely death in 2017, she taught in the MFA program at the University of Missouri-Kansas City. She was an associate editor for BkMk Press and a contributing editor of *New Letters* magazine.

BkMk Press is grateful for the support it has recently received
from the following organizations and individuals:

Missouri Arts Council
Miller-Mellor Foundation
Neptune Foundation
Richard J. Stern Foundation for the Arts
Stanley H. Durwood Foundation
William T. Kemper Foundation

Beverly Burch
Jaimee Wriston Colbert
Maija Rhee Devine
Whitney and Mariella Kerr
Carla Klausner
Lorraine M. López
Patricia Cleary Miller
Margot Patterson
Alan Proctor
James Hugo Rifenbark
Thomas Stroik
Roderick and Wyatt Townley